Hydroponic Grow Systems

Guide Book

By

KINDRA BUCK

PREFACE

THIS GUIDE WILL PROVIDE A QUICK OVERVIEW OF
HYDROPONICS AND THE SPECIFIC PROCESSES THAT
ARE USED TODAY. HERE IS A LIST OF THE THINGS YOU
WILL LEARN:

HYDROPONIC GARDENING VS. SOIL: WHAT'S THE
DIFFERENCE?
WICKING
DEEP WATER CULTURE
AEROPONICS
HYDROPONIC DRIP SYSTEMS
EBB AND FLOW
HYDROPONICS METHOD GARDENING WITH
NUTRITIONAL FILM
BEST HYDROPONIC GARDEN PLANTS
ADDITIONAL USEFUL RESOURCES

TABLE OF CONTENTS

INTRODUCTION

The world is rapidly changing, and there are no extensive grasslands. We must take care of our planet and ourselves. How better to do this than planting food in our gardens instead of grass? We can also control the pesticides and chemicals used in our food, so we know we provide our bodies with the best food. This is a great way to save money. It can be costly to buy organic produce. It is worth spending a bit to create a hydroponic system that lasts.

Continue reading to learn how you can make your dream a reality. You can create a garden that your neighbors will envy with the proper knowledge and hard work. You will be able to sleep peacefully, knowing you are doing your part in helping the environment and providing the best food for your body. It may not be as difficult as you think.

HYDROPONIC GARDENING VS. SOIL: WHAT'S THE DIFFERENCE?

Gardening is something that everyone knows. You can plant seeds, water them and then hope they grow. This method has been proven effective over thousands of years. These techniques have been improved and refined over time. For plants to thrive, they need water, air, and nutrients. Although all these tasks can be accomplished in soil, soil farming requires ample space. The number of people who need to be fed is increasing, and open areas are decreasing. What if there were a better way? Hydroponics is the future of hydroponics. Hydroponics is the cultivation of plants in water-based environments without soil. The water provides nutrients to the plants. A hydroponic system allows food to be grown indoors, outdoors, in low-soil areas, or even in space. Hydroponics offers many benefits. Hydroponics is more sustainable and produces a higher yield. Recirculating systems help to conserve water and nutrients. Plants can be grown without soil, and there is no risk of weeds, diseases, or pests like gophers and moles. These problems can be resolved, and pesticides can be removed, resulting in higher-quality, healthier fruit.

It is a great idea to create a hydroponic gardening garden indoors. But, not everyone has the space or the budget to install the lights, air conditioners, and dehumidifiers necessary inside. Other equipment. Creating a hydroponic garden in your backyard may be best for the summer.

These will be cheaper and won't take up much space in your house.

Perhaps you could take the knowledge from building an outdoor hydroponic gardening garden and create a small indoor garden in the winter. It would be a great idea to have a tower garden available during winter so your family can enjoy fresh vegetables all year.

It sounds incredible. Healthy food that uses fewer pesticides and resources on the planet. There are six main hydroponic farming methods. There are simple systems, such as deepwater culture and wicking, but also more complicated systems, like aeroponics and drip, ebb, flow, and nutrient films. Start with a more straightforward system, and then move on to a more complicated one once you are proficient. A successful gardening venture will almost always lead to other successes. Let's take a closer view of each system to determine which one is best.

WICKING

WHAT IS A WICK?

Let's get down to basics. A wicking bed is a soil-based hydroponic system. This technique, however, irrigates plants from below. It isn't easy to maintain healthy soil in a garden. It is hard to maintain healthy soil when watering from the surface. This is because much of the water is lost to evaporation. Traditional watering makes this depth challenging to achieve and almost impossible to sustain. The moisture level can be maintained constant by using a wicking mattress. When moisture levels are balanced, plants are happy.

HOW TO BUILD A WICKER BED GARDEN

1. Find the correct container for your garden. It should be sturdy, non-toxic, and water-retentive. This allows roots to grow. You can search for your house or purchase something new. You can also check social media to see if anyone is giving away a suitable container.

2. Choose a place to put the container. It is essential to place the container in a suitable spot before adding soil or water. When filled, it will be cumbersome! It must be placed where there are at least six hours of sunlight per day. It may be wise to provide afternoon shade if your area's sun is very harsh. It's a brilliant idea to place the container near water sources and where it is easy to grab dinnertime produce.

3. Level the container to ensure water is evenly distributed.

4. Insert a drip hose or tube into the container. The tube or drip hose should run from the top of the container to the bottom. This is how water will be pumped into the reservoir. You can use a robust drip hose, perforated PVC pipes, or a tile to weep. Finding an object that won't be crushed or squeezed by the soil is essential. To make water easy to add, ensure that the pipe or the hose extends from the top of your container.

5. You should place between 5-10 inches of gravel at the container's bottom. This gravel is to be covered by the pipe. It would help if you used sterile, medium-sized gravel to cover the pipe. This will ensure that there are no pathogens in your bed.

6. Cover the bed with landscape fabric to keep the soil and water reservoir from colliding. The fabric should be cut, so its edges reach the sides of the container. This will prevent soil from falling into it. Use no plastic. The soil must be able and willing to absorb the water.

7. Add a quarter inch of sand to the top of the fabric to help maintain the soil's level.

8. In your container, drill a few holes at the top of the water reservoir. This is where the soul meets the water. This will allow rainwater to flow through the container and keep the soil from becoming saturated.

9. Fill your mattress with soil. It is better to use organic, high-quality potting soil than native soil.

10. Add the plants. This is the best way to plant plants because seeds need moisture at the top of the soil.

11. Water should be poured into the reservoir. Continue along the soil line until water starts to flow out of the drilled holes.

12. Add water to the surface. This will start the wicking process. You should water the plant only for a few weeks from the top until the roots reach the soil.

13. Mulch should be spread over the soil's surface. This will reduce evaporation and keep the soil's surface cool or warm.

MAINTAINING WICKING BED

Once the plants have started to grow, an organic fertilizer will be required. You can apply the nutrients directly to the soil or add water-soluble fertilizers to the water reservoir. Both of these options could be great. If you need assistance, ask a representative at your local gardening center or refer to the instructions on the package.

Your wicking bed's water must also be kept hydrated. Water should be added once every seven days. Water should be added to the reservoir until it drains from the holes. Drain the reservoir several times per year to prevent bacteria, salt, and algae from growing. Cover the fill pipe opening with a screen if you have problems with mosquitoes. This will stop them from entering the reservoir.

Also, make sure to renew your garden's soil every year. Incorporate compost or new soil into the garden bed while it is still vacant during winter. This is necessary to preserve the soil's vitality and health. Sometimes, worms can be a welcome addition to a landscape. They thrive in moist soil. Connect a feeding tube to a "worm tower" to provide worms with nutritious and tasty food. This will make it possible to fertilize your plants.

The wicking bed is a great place to start in hydroponics. This combines traditional methods of growing plants in soil and more sustainable water techniques. This will create a better environment for plant growth and increase the plants' yield and health. It is easy to make a wicking mattress.

It is also affordable and can be enjoyed with the whole family.

DEEP WATER CULTURE

WHAT IS DEEP WATER CULTURE?

Although deep water culture sounds strange, it is one of the most effective ways to grow plants in water. It is also one of the most popular. The roots of plants in deep water culture systems float in oxygenated, nutrient-rich water. It is an all-in-one system that doesn't require much maintenance once it is set up. The plants grow faster in this water than they would in soil. There are only a few pieces to put together, and it is easy to assemble. This system, like all things, needs to be appropriately maintained, but it can be an excellent choice once it is in place.

HOW TO BUILD A SYSTEM FOR DEEP WATER CULTURE

There are many ways to build a deep-water culture system. This book is intended for beginners. Let's start with the easiest: A traditional deep-water culture system. You can buy most of the parts online, in a home improvement store, or at your local pet shop. Here's a list of items you will need.

- A 5-gallon bucket, an aquarium, or another large container

- Air Pump

- Stone Air

- Airline Tubing

- Net Pots

- We are getting Bigger (natural clay pebbles)

- Hydroponic Nutrients

- pH Control Kit

Once you have these items, you can begin to make your deep water culture system.

1. Connect the tube to your air pump

2. Connect the tube to the air stone

3. Place the stone of Air in the bucket

4. Add water to the bucket.

5. Make sure you know the pH of your water. Plants prefer soil pH between 5.5 to 6. 5. Keep an eye on the pH and note that it can change as plants grow. The pH should be higher when plants grow but lower when they are flowering.

6. Place food in the water. There are many ways to get nutrients. Talk to your local garden center staff to find the best option for you. You can start with the General Hydroponics Flora Series.

Because it is simple to use, you can mix different amounts at different stages in the plant's development by following the instructions.

7. Start your seeds. This is a crucial step in the process. To prevent algae growth, it is a good idea to tape the sides and bottom of your container if they are not too dark. The seed should be placed in the medium for growth, and the entire thing should go into the pot. The roots should begin to grow in seven to 14 days.

8. It will be fantastic to see the speed at which roots grow once they touch the water. The plant can survive underwater as long as it has enough food and oxygen.

Traditional methods are an excellent place to start. If this method is unsuitable, consider making a recirculating water culture system. The system allows the same plant can be grown in multiple buckets. All buckets receive their nutrient solution in one reservoir.

MAINTAINING A HEALTHY DEEP WATER CULTURE SYSTEM.

This system can have some problems. It can take time to master pH, water level, and nutrient concentration. These numbers can also change in a small system. Another thing that could go wrong is the power going out. The roots could "swim away" if the pump fails or the oxygen level drops in the solution. Temperature can also pose a problem. Water should be kept between 60 and 68 degrees. The oxygen level drops as the temperature rises. If the water temperature is too low, the plant may think it's winter or fall and then die.

If they are kept in top shape and observed, most problems can be resolved quickly. Every so often, the nutrient solution should be changed. The entire solution should be replaced at least once every three weeks. It will take some research to determine how often this should happen. It all depends on the type of plants being grown, the size of the reservoir, and the stage in which the plants are in their growth cycles.

You should also be aware of the presence of diseases or underwater roots. Make sure that no part of the stem or leaves gets wet. An inch and a quarter should allow roots to rise above the waterline. The airstone should create bubbles at the top to prevent roots from drying. It would help if you also kept an eye on the plants to ensure they look healthy. Pythium can be fatal to plants.

This system may take some time to find the best place for you. The sun is the best light source for plants. It might be challenging to maintain the water temperature in direct sunlight, mainly if there is a lot of sun in the yard. You could move the system on wheels or place it in a sunroom, greenhouse, or window. You may have to use artificial lights if the system works only inside.

AEROPONICS

WHAT IS AEROPONICS?

Aeroponics is a method that allows plants to be grown in the air. The plants are not growing in soil or water. They are instead exposed to a moist environment rich in nutrients. The system can be used indoors, outdoors, or in a greenhouse. You can choose from high-pressure or low-pressure hydroponic systems. High-pressure systems require fewer resources and are more sophisticated. NASA has used these systems to grow vegetables. These systems can be expensive for those who garden in their backyards. Low-pressure systems are the best option for people who want to build their projects.

HOW TO BUILD AN AEROPONIC SYSTEM.

 Although you can buy ready-to-go aeroponic systems, it is cheaper to make your own. There are many ways to make a plant system in the air. You can grow plants in a 5-gallon bucket, a tower garden, or many other places. The book only covers one method of building, but you can find other methods online. This will be done using a plastic bag that can hold 30 gallons.

What you'll need:

- (1) A dark 30-gallon container with a lid.
- The hydroponic net pots have lids made from rubber foam. The size and quantity of plants will vary depending on their size.
- A timer with an electric motor can be set to increments of 30 minutes.
- PVC pipe (3/4 inch)
- (6) 34-inch PVC slip connectors.
- (1) 34" "cross-on" PVC connector.
- (2) PVC connector for 34-inch "T" slip.
- (6) PVC connectors with a 34-inch slip to a 1/2" thread.
- (1) 34-inch "T-" slip connector with a 1/2-inch threaded top.
- (1) Silicone-based caulking tube.
- (1) Stop valve for 1/2 inch Flexi-tubing
- (1) Bulkhead fitting, 1/2-inch thread, and gasket.
- (1) 1/2" hose clamp
- (1) Black 12-inch Flexi-tubing.
- (1) Male threaded connector to fit a 1/2 inch barb.
- (6) 12-inch plastic sprinkler heads with threads 180 degrees.
- (1) Fountain pump (200 Gallons/Hour).

1. Your plastic tote should have a lid holding 30 gallons. A darker color is the best way to prevent algae growth. It would help if you also collected your net pots. These will vary in size depending on the plant you are trying to grow.

Pots with a height of 3.75 inches would be ideal for tomatoes. If your crop is small, choose something smaller or more substantial if it's enormous. To allow your net pots to fit inside the tote's cover, you must make holes in its lid. These holes can be cut with a craft knife.

2. A 3'4" length of 34-inch PVC pipe. You should ensure you get PVC and NOT CPVC, as CPVC can release harmful chemicals. The following should be done to the pipe:

- (6) 4.5" lengths.
- (6) 6-inch lengths
- Length: 8
- Three-inch lengths

3. Use primer and PVC glue to attach the 6" and 4.5" lengths. These connectors will look similar to the letter L. The 4.5-inch length will lie flat on the ground, and the 6-inch length will rise into the air.

4. Attach the 34-inch slip to the 12-inch threaded PVC connector at the top of every 6" pipe in the "L" shape. Install sprinkler heads now.

5. Two 34" PVC T connectors and one 34-inch cross connector are required. To join the "L"-shaped pipes, use PVC primer and glue. Two sets can be connected using the "T" and one set using the "cross."

6. Your PVC pipe creation can be pictured in your tote, with water spraying up at the roots. Connect the 8-inch piece of PVC pipe to the end of the "T" connector. Add one of the 3" sections to the other end of the "cross connector," then

attach the "T" connector with the opening facing straight up. Next, add another 3" section and glue it into the existing "T" connector.

7. Attach a 1/2 inch barb to the 1/2" threaded connector to the sticking part of the "T" connector.

8. Place the sprinkler in the bag. Attach the 1/2-inch Flexi tubing to the fountain pump. You must ensure that the tubing is free from kinks.

9. Cover the lid with caulk and place it back on top. Make sure the caulking is completely dry before you use it.

10. Attach the bulkhead fitting at the bottom of your tote, and then use Flexi-tubing to connect the drain and shut-off valves.

11. Place plants in the net pots. Fill the net pots with water and set the timer to 25 minutes and 25 minutes off. Your plants can be helped to grow by feeding them.

A humidity dome can be used to help young cuttings grow.

HOW TO CARE FOR AN AEROPONICS SYSTEM

An aeroponic system is just like any other system. It is important to ensure that the pump works properly. The plants will suffer if the pump is not working properly. Sprinkler heads can become clogged from the nutrients. These can also cause sprinkler heads to become clogged. To keep them clean, you should be keeping an eye on them and using isopropyl alcohol every now and again. The sprinkler heads might need to be replaced if the problem becomes too severe before it is noticed.

There are many ways to prevent bacteria and mold growth in these systems. Because the environment is humid and warm, this happens frequently. Use a small amount hydrogen peroxide to kill the bacteria. This will kill any good bacteria and fungi found in your supplements.

Plant roots grow best in darkness. It is important that the box does not get sunlight. Each hole must be sealed. The roots of a plant require complete darkness while the rest of it does not. You can either provide enough light or use artificial lighting if you are setting this up inside. The whole system is lightweight and compact so it's a good option for those who live in apartments and want to put it on the deck, then bring it inside when the temperature drops.

HYDROPONIC DRIP SYSTEMS

WHAT IS THE DRIP SYSTEM FOR HYDROPONICS?

The most popular method to grow plants is the hydroponic drip system. Hydroponic drip systems work similarly to regular soil drip irrigation systems. It provides a water-based nutrition solution for plants' roots. This system works well, even though it has a slow flow rate. The water slowly drips at the plants' base, so there is little evaporation. It is almost like rain falling from heaven. People who live in apartments or want to grow their food and large commercial farms can use this system. It works as a natural process and is extremely effective.

It is simple to set up. You can use it to grow plants in individual pots or vertically. You can save space if you live in an apartment. Only a drip emitter must be at the vertical system's top end. The water flows down, watering plants as it goes. It reaches the bottom and returns to the reservoir.

There are two types of hydroponic drip systems. Systems that can recover water and those that don't. A recovery system allows the nutrient solution to be passed through the system multiple times. This recycled solution is a cost-saving option for nutrients and water but requires more monitoring and care. The water thrown out will have a different pH, and nutrient level as the plants use it. This could mean that the pH level needs to be adjusted, or the nutrient solution might need to be drained.

Non-recovery systems send the solution once. Although this may seem wasteful, they are often more effective. This can only be achieved if drip cycles are precise. You can use almost every drop of the solution by setting timers for each plant and creating a drip. The solution can't be reused so the reservoir should only be filled with a new solution.

There is no need for you to monitor the pH or nutrient levels like in recovery systems.

Overall, it's a simple system with few moving parts. If the power goes out or something goes wrong, other systems will not work. This system is very versatile and can be used for many purposes. You can use it on a small balcony or in a large business. Hydroponic drip systems can support large plants such as squash and melons. Most other systems can only support smaller plants.

HOW TO MAKE A HYDROPONIC GARDEN DRIP SYSTEM

 You can purchase a kit like most systems. However, it's more fun and cost-effective to build your own. These are the items you will need and information on how to set it up.

1. Choose the correct container. There are several ways to go about this. There are several options: you can place all your plants in one pot, separate pots to accommodate different types of plants, and a smaller pot for each plant. Whatever pot you use, ensure that the nutrient solution drains out of the bottom.

2. Make sure it is easy to grow. The plants must be supported by something that can hold water and air and let enough water drain away. River rocks can be placed at the bottom of grow containers. You can also use coco coir, clay aggregate, and rockwool as media around the plants.

3. You will need a container that can hold the nutrient solution. It should be dark and closed so that light cannot get through. This is to prevent bacteria and algae from growing and causing problems. Place the reservoir in a convenient place and then fill it up.

4. Get submersible pumps. There are many options for submersible pumps. You can use a pump from a pond or fountain, or you could consider an aquarium pump. You can add an airstone to ensure that the roots receive enough oxygen. This will allow the roots to absorb more nutrients and aid in faster growth.

5. Give the pump a timer. It will allow the pump to be turned on and off several times daily. This is not something that most people need to know. If the plan calls to create a complex, non-recovery system that is as efficient as possible, it will likely require a cycle time.

6. You can look around, or visit the store, to find irrigation fittings and tubing. There are many options available depending on the purpose of the irrigation system. You can use PVC, flexible tubing or thin spaghetti tubing. You will need one drip emitter or nozzle to reach each plant. To get to each plant, you could lay some tubing with holes punched in it. This is an easy way to accomplish it.

A vertical garden is an excellent idea if you don't have much space. These can even be made from recycled items like plastic bottles. These can be made with soil and regular water or using growing media and a drip-system. You can place a drip on each plant or at the top of the plant and let the water flow to the bottom.

HOW TO KEEP A HYDROPONIC DRIP SYSTEMS RUNNING

It is essential to maintain the drip emitters in this system. Hydroponic drip systems can be prone to clogging. If the dripper tips get clogged with minerals or algae, or if the liquid solution is too thick, this can cause the emitters to become clogged. You can prevent these problems by checking the emitters frequently and tapping them to remove any sediment. Pay attention to the pH level of the nutrient solution. To ensure that nutrients are adequately dissolved, read the instructions carefully. Clean everything thoroughly between growing cycles. Clean the growing medium with nitric acid. This will stop bacteria and algae growth.

This system has its problems. The emitters can get clogged. It is also challenging to keep an eye on recovery systems' pH and nutrient levels. This system is flexible and easy to use. You can set up an area like this in your yard, deck, or kitchen. There are many possibilities.

EBB AND FLOW

WHAT IS "EBB & FLOW"?

Flood and drain are another term for ebb-flow. This system delivers water, food, oxygen, and oxygen to the roots of plants in cycles. After the water and nutrients have dried, they are poured onto the growing area. The growing medium is affected by rain, and it gets wet. However, it can dry before it rains again. Because the plant's roots must grow to get water, this works out well. The root system of a plant is the most important thing. It absorbs nutrients better and will grow faster.

This intermediate system is prevalent. This system is popular due to its simplicity and affordability. It can be built small or large for small spaces or large for larger ones. The nutrient solution is able to pass through the system multiple times, making it very efficient. It is not thrown out after one trip. The system can also run independently for many days or weeks if everything is in order. Make sure everything is in the right stage of growth.

This system can also support plants of medium-large size. The ebb-and-flow system is excellent for tomatoes, beans, and cucumbers. They like to have their roots dry when they are flowering or making fruit.

MAKING A SYSTEM WITH EBBS & FLOWS

This system can be built in many ways, or you can buy them pre-assembled. You can go crazy and get a table with a tray. This can look great and serve its purpose well. Plastic bins are a great place to start for beginners. This system is very affordable and will allow you to familiarize yourself with each part's operation before you upgrade.

Here is a list of things you will need:

- Totes or storage bins 16-20 gallons in black or dark colors
- Clear 30 quart tote (30 quarts) (This should be about the same height as the lid of the darker-colored tote).

- A garden timer that can run for up to 15 minutes.
- Aquarium air pump.
- You will find 6 feet of tube, and a "T" connector.
- Air stone 5."
- Four flower pots measuring 8 inches tall were used in this system. If you prefer smaller pots, you can add more.
- It comes in a small pouch.
- Black irrigation tubing measuring approximately 18 inches in diameter with a 1/2 inch inside diameter.
- A small pond pump that can go underwater (120 gph). Set of fittings to fill and drain the pond with one extension. It is better to buy a kit specifically designed for an ebb-flow system. These can be ordered online.
- Brick made from coconut fiber
- LECA in a small bag. (Hydroton clay balls).
- pH test kit.
- How many bottles of nutrient concentration do you need.

Tools Required:

- Power drill.
- Hole saw.
- 3/8" spade or regular drill bit

 Ask your friends if they have the tools or purchase them. These tools are great if you're interested in hydroponics.

Instructions:

1. Two 14-inch holes should be made in the middle and sides of the clear tote. These holes should be close to one another, and the pots should be placed around them.

2. Place the clear tray over the lid of the other container. Place it in the middle. Mark the exact center of the holes on the black lid with a marker. Two 1 14 inch holes should be cut in the black lid so that they line up with the clear tray.

3. Make two holes in the black lid, each one the same size (14 inches). The first should be in the center of the far right, and the second in the upper left corner. The pump plug and bubbler tube must pass through one of these holes, while the other hole is used to add nutrient solution and check the water level.

4. Attach your drain fittings to the bin's centers. The rubber seal is located at the bottom of your bin. You don't need tools to turn them. Place the extension on the tube to make the overflow tube (the thicker tube is the one).

Next, install the pump. Next, place the 1/2" irrigation tubing on top of the outlet fitting. You might need to attach a zip tie to secure the irrigation tubing if it doesn't fit well. You can use a razor blade to make a hole in the tube if it is too tight.

6. Place the clear tray over the black lid. Place the drain fittings on the tray. The drain fittings must be in the correct place and pass through the lid.

7. The reservoir is where you place the pump. Connect the black tube to the drain tube's port. The tubing must be cut to be straight when the lid's on. You should measure, cut, and test it before you can call it done. Once the tube is at the correct length, place it on the drain tube. To ensure it fits snugly, attaches a zip tie. It is very important that the tube remains in place.

8. Place the bubbler stone into the bottom of the

black/dark tee, and then push the tubing up through the access hole at the previously drilled side.

9. Place the top and click it in place.

10. Make a "dipstick" with a wooden or stick dowel. This will allow you to measure the solution in your reservoir without needing to remove the lid. Adding water to the reservoir would help if you marked the "dipstick" as a 2 gallons marker.

11. Place the set-up on a flat surface. The reservoir holds 10 gallons of water. Make sure to mark the "dipstick" every time you add 2 Gallons of water. Next, add the nutrient concentrate that you have chosen. You can use Flora Micro, Flora Grow, or Flora Bloom. To do this, you will need to add ten teaspoons each.

12. To change the pH of your solution, use your test kit

13. Test the system by plugging the bubbler into the pump. Check that everything is working as it should and that there are no leaks.

14. It's now time to plant the plants. You can check to ensure the pots will fit in the trash bin.

15. Each pot should have several holes 14 inches or 3/8 inches around its bottom. This will allow the nutrient solution to drain correctly.

16. Place your hydroponics medium into the pots. The good idea is to put a few inches of LECA (Hydroton or clay balls) at the bottom of each pot. The more considerable material prevents the medium from escaping the drain holes and is a good sublayer

overall. Fill the remainder of the pot with a mixture of perlite and coco coir. This mixture works well at holding water but lets air in.

17. Place the seedlings into the pots. Make sure that the soil is tight around them to ensure they stay in place. Because the water doesn't reach the top, the ebb-and-flow system cannot be used to plant seeds. They would not be able to get enough water for seeds to grow. There are several ways to get your plants started. You can either start them in grow cubes and pellets or buy seedlings in a shop. After washing the roots, place them in pots.

18. The first few days after planting, water them from the top to help them adjust to the new place in the ebb-and-flow system. You should also watch the system closely to ensure everything is working correctly. The pots should be lifted if there is still water in the tray at the end of the drain cycle. The roots will rot if they are

left in water for too long. Place something underneath to lift the pots about 12 inches off the ground. Plastic is a good choice and does not add chemicals to the system.

19. The timer can be connected to the water pump. The system will fill the tank thrice daily for 15 minutes each. It's a good idea to fill in at six o'clock in the morning, noon, or six p.m. The plants like to sleep at night, so don't bother them.

20. The bubbler pump and air stone should be left all day. This allows the nutrient solution to breathe and prevents it from going stale.

You can give your plants the best lighting by placing them in a sunny window during the day or outside. A light is required if the plant will be indoors and not near windows.

HYDROPONICS METHOD GARDENING WITH NUTRITIONAL FILM

WHAT IS NUTRIENT FILM TECHNIQUE HYDROPONIC GARDENS AND WHAT ARE THEY?

Hydroponic gardening: Technique of the Nutrient Film This technique is similar to the flow and ebb of water. Instead of draining away the nutrients, they are constantly recirculated around the roots. This is due to gravity, which is a marvelous phenomenon. It is important that water flows down the tray by being placed at an angle. Water can be pushed into the top of the tray and then drained from the bottom.

The roots are treated with nutrient film techniques by applying a thin layer of fertilizer solution. They contain a lot of food, but not all of it is absorbed. The roots' top areas, which are kept dry, have a lot of oxygen and air. This method is best for plants with low growth rates and low weight. Trellises are required to support larger plants such as grapevines. This configuration is not suitable for top-heavy plants, as the roots hang free and are not supported by any growing medium.

HOW TO PUT TOGETHER A NUTRIENT FILM HYDRAPOONIC GARDEN

There are many ways to build your own hydroponic garden using nutrient films. A tray can be used to build smaller systems similar to the ebb-flow system. These can be used inside or outside, on a deck, or in any other small area. Next, you will find instructions to make a large-scale outdoor system. You can transform your backyard into an agricultural farm if you make several of these.

Here is a list of things you will need:

- (8) 2x4s measuring 8 feet in length

- Sawhorse brackets number 3.

- (18) Curved plant hangers made from metal with screws

- (8) 10-foot-long pieces of PVC pipe 3" in diameter.

- Shorter 3" PVC sweep elbow.

- End cap for 3 inch PVC pipe.

- 6 feet of black 14 inch tube

- The reservoir will consist of a 70-gallon container and a lid. Submersible pump (550gph).

- Pump bag 10 inches

- (120) 2" netcups.

- (122) 1.5-inch rockwool plugs, accelaroot starter sticks, or any other medium sufficient to fill (120) 2-inch net pots.

Tools Required:

- Drill. 1.5"

- Self-feeding bit

Do some research to find out more about the nutrients you want in your body. FloraGro and FloraMicro are good options.

Instructions:

1. You will have three sets of Aframes if you connect the 2x4s and the brackets on your sawhorses.

2. You will need to dig holes wherever you want the system. The A-frame sets should not be more than 3.5 feet apart. Each A-frame's leg should be buried about one foot below the ground using an angle.

3. Attach one of each set of A-frames to the other 2x4s. This will hold everything in place and provide a solid base for your work.

4. Screw the plant hangers from metal into the A Frame sets at a gradual angle not exceeding 2 percent. This will ensure that water doesn't rush through the system.

5. Make holes in the PVC pipe about 6 inches apart that are 1.5 inches in diameter. This will prevent the net pots of 2 inches from falling through the holes. When it's finished, there should be approximately 120 holes.

6. The hooks can be used to hang the PVC pipes. They may need to be cut once they reach the A-frame's end. The sweep elbows can be used to connect the pipes while they travel down the A-frame. To prevent leakage, you might use waterproof PVC glue to attach the pipes to the elbows.

7.Tighten your short sweep elbow until you reach the end pipe at the end. This will be inserted into the water tank.

8. Make a hole of 14 inches in the end cap.

9. Connect the other end of the 14-inch tubing to the pump by inserting one end into the hole. Place the pump in the bag. Make sure that the tubing and pump cord pass through the hole at the top of your reservoir.

10. Cover the port of the reservoir cover using the short sweep elbow. This will allow the water to return to the reservoir. You might want to bury the reservoir in order to keep the reservoir's solution from being affected by summer heat. This should be kept cool.

11. Add water and nutrient solutions to the water tank. Check the pH of the water tank and adjust it as necessary. After plugging in the pump, test the system to ensure it is functioning properly.

12. Place one net pot into each hole, and then add some seedlings or other medium. This system doesn't allow water to reach the top of the pot so it is not possible to grow seeds from them. Some plants might need additional watering every few days to get going.

MAINTAINING A NUTRIENT FILM TECHNIQUE HYDROPONIC GARDEN

This method is best for plants with small root systems. Greens and herbs are the best options. Large plants and plants will clog it with substantial root systems. Either buy seeds from a nursery or start your own seeds. You can wash the roots of seedlings purchased from a garden centre by gently washing them. It will then be ready for you to put in the growing medium. The roots should be long enough so that they reach the nutrient films.

The Hydroponic Garden System should be run continuously, day and night. The reservoir should be cleaned and refilled with new nutrient solutions every two to four weeks. Between these intervals, you should be monitoring the pH and nutrient levels of the water. You should also eliminate old plants with large roots that can clog the system. This will allow plants to grow fast and well. Because it has 120 holes, this system will produce a high yield. You can plant many different things to ensure you don't have a freezer that is only one.

BEST HYDROPONIC GARDEN PLANTS

The type of vegetables that you are trying to grow will often determine which system you should use. Some systems work best with larger plants, while others require smaller plants. Consider which vegetables you and your family love the most, and which ones are most frequently bought at the grocery store. You should probably start right here. You can grow a lot of food with hydroponic gardening, so make sure you choose the foods you love. Think about how vegetables taste fresher when picked fresh. Your own tomatoes taste better than the ones you buy from the grocery store. Root vegetables purchased at the store aren't much better than those grown in your garden.

Avoid plants that take up too much space. Squash, zucchini, melons and corn love to spread out. All will be theirs. This holds true even if you garden indoors, on a deck, or in a small area. You can support your vines and allow them to grow to the ceiling in your garden or greenhouse.

Five plants do exceptionally well in a hydroponics system. These are the best plants to start with if you've never grown plants in water. You can then move on to other items once you have mastered how to use them.

LETTUCE (AND OTHER GREENS)

Salad is on the horizon! Leafy greens are the best thing to grow in hydroponic systems. The roots of the plants aren't deep and don't grow tall. The plants do not need to be supported. These plants also increase, so you can pick some lettuce each day and make a salad. You can plant different types of lettuce at different times to ensure that you have plenty of lettuce on hand. It takes around 30 days for lettuce to grow. The best pH range is between 6.0-7.0. There are wide suitable varieties, including Bibb, Boston, Buttercrunch and Buttercrunch.

If you grow them outdoors, ensure they are in direct sunlight for long periods. If you are growing them indoors, ensure they get light for at least 18 hours. You can move the lights around as the plant grows. However, keep the lights at 6 inches above the plant. Varieties like Yolo Wonder, Ace, Vidi, and California Wonder are possible.

HERBS

Hydroponics is a beautiful way to get started. They can be used in any system. You can choose many herbs, making it easy to fill every pot with the right kind.

Many people believe that hydroponic herbs taste better than those grown in soil. After you have decided what you want to grow, you will need to find out the growth time and pH. Watercress, basil, and parsley can all be used. You can also use other herbs to make your dishes. To grow herbs in hydroponic systems, flush the medium once per week to remove any nutrients the plants haven't taken in.

ADDITIONAL USEFUL RESOURCES

It is amazing what you can find online these days. Hydroponics is a fascinating subject that you can research before you begin. The book showed you how to make each system by yourself. You can find many ready-made solutions and other ways to accomplish the same thing. It is easy to find information about the plant you wish to grow, such as tips and pH levels.

Make friends at your local garden center by meeting up with someone. Ask around to discover someone who is knowledgeable about hydroponic gardening. It can be very helpful to have someone nearby to answer your questions and show you the ropes in person. Hydroponic gardening is something anyone can get interested in once they can share what they have learned.

These are some additional details on how lighting works in hydroponic systems. The sun is the best light source, as we have already stated.

The sun is the best light source for plants. They need to get 4 to 6 hours of direct sunshine and 8 to 10 hours of bright sunlight.

You need to ensure that your hydroponic system works properly. It's great to have your hydroponic system outside. If you don't have a window, you can purchase a variety of lights. These are just a few to consider.

T5 FLUORESCENT LASPS

These lights are among the most affordable for hydroponics. They also run calmly and quietly. These lights are great for ornamental houseplants, herbs, or leafy vegetables such as Spinach and lettuce. These lights can be used to start cuttings, seeds, or clones. If you are looking to grow seeds indoors, this light could be the right one to purchase. They are not suitable for growing flowers or vegetables that produce fruit, as they lack enough light.

These lights can be used in a variety of ways. They should be kept between 4 and 6 inches from the plants. They will not burn the plants as they run cool. You should have 40 watts for each square foot of your planting bed. A good rule of thumb is to use one 4-foot tube per two square feet.

HIGH-INTENSITY DISCHARGE SYSTEMS (HID)

These bright lights have been used in commercial greenhouses for many decades. They are now easy to find and work well in hydroponics gardens at home. HID lighting systems provide plants with the right spectrum to grow fruits and flowers. It works in the same way as what the sun does outside. These lights can get very hot and expensive.

Two HID bulbs are available: metal halide (MH) and high-pressure sodium (HPS). While most vegetables will grow well under an HID light at any stage of their life, an HPS light is more beneficial for flowering or fruiting plants. While it is more efficient, it is not essential. A metal halide is a good option if you have only one light. These bulbs can last many years, despite being expensive.

GROW LIGHTS WITH LIGHT EMITTING DIODES (LEDS),

This new technology was not suitable for grow lights until recently. These lights are more expensive upfront, but they last longer, use less electricity, are cooler, and last much longer. Pay attention to what you purchase. While some LED lights are cheap enough to be used for growing, they don't often have the spectrums required for hydroponic gardening.

You should, at the minimum, buy a 5-band, or 7-band, mid-range LED panel. A high-end LED grow lamp will produce the best results. California Lightworks SolarSystem 550 might be something you want to consider.

You can choose how to light your hydroponic gardens.

Plants that grow in water require 16 substances. The air is the only way to get carbon, hydrogen, or oxygen. However, the 13 other elements must be obtained from a nutrient solution. This group includes 13 elements: molybdenum (copper), manganese and iron, copper, zinc, boron and zinc, and manganese as well as manganese, iron, calcium, magnesium, potassium, phosphorous, phosphorous, and nitrogen. There are many solutions. While this book has covered a few of the best, some gardeners make their own.

CONCLUSION

We appreciate you taking the time to read DIY Hydroponics For Beginners: The Essential Guide for Turning Your Backyard into A Farm. We hope you have gained a solid foundational understanding of hydroponics.

Next, think about the book and create a plan. You might be surprised at what you have that you can use to build a hydroponics system. Think about the types of plants that you would like to grow, and which system is best for them. You should also consider where the hydroponic garden will be placed. Is it really worth converting your entire backyard into a farm? Can you do hydroponic gardening in a window or on your balcony right now?

Once you have a plan and a plan for building a system, do some more research. Ask your friends on social media if they have any experience in this field. Go to a local store that sells hydroponic gardening products. You can ask any questions you have and help get things started.

The world is rapidly changing. It is time to think about ways to grow food more sustainably. These systems have been proven to be very successful by many commercial farms. You can grow more food on less land and with less water. Hydroponic systems allow people to grow plants with fewer pesticides and chemicals. If you choose how plants are grown, you can control what goes into the body.

Hydroponic gardening is a relaxing hobby. Get back in touch and enjoy nature after a long day or week of work. Go home after sitting in traffic for hours and take a moment to check on your plants. When you see the difference in their growth, smile.

This is another hobby the whole family can enjoy. Spend time planning and building your garden together. Discuss the foods everyone enjoys and discuss which vegetables to plant from seeds. You will be amazed at how happy your children are when their plants begin to grow and produce fruits.

It's an excellent opportunity to share your knowledge with your children and teach them how you fix any problems that may arise. You can learn a lot from hydroponic gardening. Finally, everyone will be proud to enjoy a meal prepared with fresh produce from the garden. The best times are shared with family around the dinner table.

Thank you for purchasing our travel guide book! We hope you're enjoying it and finding it useful.

We would like to thank you in advance if you decide to go ahead and book your holiday. If you are satisfied with the book, we would appreciate it if you left a review. This allows us to keep providing fantastic travel content and aids other people in making educated travel decisions.